6 10 14 20 22 26 30

34 38 40 42 46 50

Number stickers for activity on page 31

10 15 25 35 45

Number stickers for activity on page 32

20 30 50 70 90

Number stickers for activity on page 33

School Skills

Addition and Subtraction

PaRRagon

Bath • New York • Singapore • Hong Kong • Cologne • Delhi
Melbourne • Amsterdam • Johannesburg • Auckland • Shenzhen

This edition published by Parragon in 2010

Parragon
Queen Street House
4 Queen Street
Bath BA1 1HE, UK

ISBN 978-1-4454-1706-6

Printed in China

Dear Parent,

Disney School Skills Workbooks are the perfect tools to make a difference in your child's learning. Inside this book, you'll find a developmental progression of activities designed to help your child master essential skills critical for school success. Interactive stickers help improve your child's speed and accuracy with basic addition and subtraction.

Why is quick and automatic recall of basic math facts important? Research shows these skills are necessary to improve a child's abilities for mental computation and estimation. Learning fact strategies helps a child memorize maths facts more efficiently and then organize those facts into groups, such as sums of tens, turn-around facts, doubles and so on.

As a child gains proficiency in his or her ability to recall maths facts, they are better able to spend more time on problem solving. They don't need to stop and count. Frequent practice now will prepare your child for more complex maths computation later on.

As partners in learning with Disney School Skills Workbooks, you can help your child reach important milestones to become a confident and independent learner.

Let's Learn Math Facts

It's a fact! You need to know your maths facts. This book will give you lots of practice using fact strategies. You'll find stickers and lots more to help you learn addition and subtraction facts F-A-S-T.

Improve your speed and accuracy with lots of practice!

Count on when 1, 2 or 3 is added.
5 plus 2 more is 5, 6, 7.

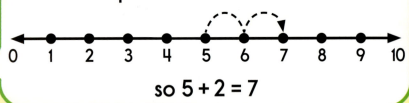

so 5 + 2 = 7

Count back when 1, 2, or 3 is subtracted.
5 take away 2 is 5, 4, 3.

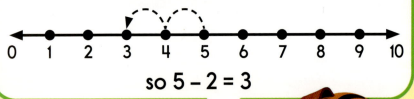

so 5 − 2 = 3

Know your turn-arounds!
I repeat! Know your turn-arounds
now! Knowing turn-around facts
cuts the numbers of facts you
need to know in half.
If you know 3 + 5 = 8,
then you also know 5 + 3 = 8.

Get to know your
fact families.

$2 + 3 = 5$ $5 - 3 = 2$
$3 + 2 = 5$ $5 - 2 = 3$

Knowing doubles and doubles plus one
gives you fact power.

$5 + 5 = 10$ $5 + 6 = 11$

For MORE fact power, use
doubles and doubles-plus-one facts
to find differences!

$10 - 5 = 5$ $11 - 5 = 6$

I think adding or
subtracting zero is easy.
Is it easy for you?
Tell me honestly.

$9 + 0 = 9$ $12 + 0 = 12$
$9 - 0 = 9$ $12 - 0 = 12$

5

Let's Show Different Ways to Make 7, 8, 9, 10, 11, 12

Colour the circles blue and yellow.
Show two different ways to make the number.
The first one is done for you.

7	● ● ● ● ◯ ◯ ◯ __4__ and __3__
7	◯ ◯ ◯ ◯ ◯ ◯ ◯ ___ and ___
8	◯ ◯ ◯ ◯ ◯ ◯ ◯ ◯ ___ and ___
8	◯ ◯ ◯ ◯ ◯ ◯ ◯ ◯ ___ and ___
9	◯ ◯ ◯ ◯ ◯ ◯ ◯ ◯ ◯ ___ and ___
9	◯ ◯ ◯ ◯ ◯ ◯ ◯ ◯ ◯ ___ and ___

10	○○○○○○○○○○ **and** ___ ___
10	○○○○○○○○○○ **and** ___ ___
11	○○○○○○○○○○○ **and** ___ ___
11	○○○○○○○○○○○ **and** ___ ___
12	○○○○○○○○○○○○ **and** ___ ___
12	○○○○○○○○○○○○ **and** ___ ___

Let's Add

Read the problem.
Write the answer.
The first one is done for you.

There are 2 .

Woody gets 2 more.

How many in all?

_2_ and _2_ more is _4_ .

There are 5 .

Woody gets 1 more.

How many in all?

___ and ___ more is ___ .

There are 4 .

Buzz gets 2 more.

How many in all?

___ and ___ more is ___ .

There are 6 .

Bo Peep gets 3 more.

How many in all?

___ and ___ more is ___ .

There are 7 .

Rex gets 2 more.

How many in all?

___ and ___ more is ___ .

There are 4 🔴 .

Woody gets 3 more.

How many in all?

___ and ___ more is ___ .

There are 6 🔵 .

Buzz gets 4 more.

How many in all?

___ and ___ more is ___ .

There are 7 ⭐ .

Bo Peep gets 4 more.

How many in all?

___ and ___ more is ___ .

There are 7 ⭐ .

Rex gets 3 more.

How many in all?

___ and ___ more is ___ .

Write your own maths story.

There are ☐ balls.

Rex gets ☐ more.

How many in all?

☐ and ☐ more is ☐ .

Let's Count On to Add

4 plus 3.
Start at 4.
Count on 3:
4...5, 6, **7**

Count on to add.
Write the sum.
The first one is done for you.

0 1 2 3 4 5 6 7 8 9 10 11 12

$$4 + 3 = \boxed{7}$$

$$6 + 2 = \square$$

$$3 + 2 = \square$$

$$\begin{array}{r} 4 \\ + 2 \\ \hline \square \end{array}$$

$$\begin{array}{r} 5 \\ + 1 \\ \hline \square \end{array}$$

$$\begin{array}{r} 3 \\ + 3 \\ \hline \square \end{array}$$

Use the number line.
Count on to add.
Write the sum.

← 0 1 2 3 4 5 6 7 8 9 10 11 12 →

6
+1
☐

7
+2
☐

10
+2
☐

5 + 3 = ☐

8 + 3 = ☐

9 + 3 = ☐

11 + 1 = ☐

Let's Add 0

Write the sum.

4 + 0 = ☐

0 + 8 = ☐

0 + 5 = ☐

12 + 0 = ☐

0 + 11 = ☐

4 + 0 = ☐

$$9 + 0 = \boxed{}$$

$$0 + 7 = \boxed{}$$

$$6 + 0 = \boxed{}$$

$$3 + 0 = \boxed{}$$

Adding 0 does not change a number!

⭐ **Super-Duper Problem:**

500 + 0 = ☐

Let's Add Doubles

Write the sum.

$0 + 0 = \boxed{}$

$2 + 2 = \boxed{}$

$3 + 3 = \boxed{}$

$4 + 4 = \boxed{}$

$6 + 6 = \boxed{}$

$8 + 8 = \boxed{}$

$\begin{array}{r} 5 \\ + 5 \\ \hline \boxed{} \end{array}$

$\begin{array}{r} 7 \\ + 7 \\ \hline \boxed{} \end{array}$

$\begin{array}{r} 9 \\ + 9 \\ \hline \boxed{} \end{array}$

$\begin{array}{r} 10 \\ + 10 \\ \hline \boxed{} \end{array}$

★ **Super-Duper Problems:**

$100 + 100 = \boxed{}$

$1000 + 1000 = \boxed{}$

13

Let's Add with 5

Add the checkers.
Write the sum.
The first one is done for you.

5 + 3 = __8__

5 + 1 = ___

5 + 2 = ___

5 + 4 = ___

5 + 0 = ___

Let's Add

Colour the checkers.
Write the sum.
The first one is done for you.

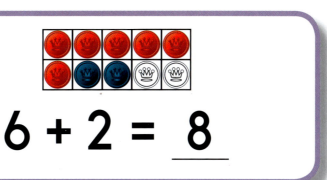

6 + 2 = __8__

7 + 1 = ___

6 + 3 = ___

8 + 1 = ___

7 + 2 = ___

Let's Race

Solve the problems.
Record your time and the
number of correct answers.
On your mark, get set, go!

6 + 4	7 + 3	5 + 6	2 + 9	4 + 2
3 + 3	8 + 4	3 + 6	6 + 3	0 + 8
9 + 3	6 + 6	8 + 3	2 + 3	7 + 2
1 + 3	6 + 0	3 + 4	3 + 2	1 + 7
6 + 2	4 + 5	10 + 2		

Time to Complete: _____

Total Answers: _____

Total Correct: _____

Solve the problems.
Record your time and the
number of correct answers.
On your mark, get set, go!

4 + 1	7 + 5	0 + 2	2 + 4	3 + 0
4 + 7	2 + 7	1 + 6	4 + 3	8 + 1
1 + 1	8 + 2	5 + 3	7 + 4	2 + 2
5 + 5	1 + 2	5 + 7	4 + 6	0 + 7
10 + 1	5 + 1	4 + 4	Time to Complete: _____ Total Answers: _____ Total Correct: _____	

17

Let's Subtract

Read the problem.
Write the difference.
The first one is done for you.

There are 3 .

2 bounce away.

How many are left?

__3__ take away __2__ is __1__ .

There are 4 .

2 bounce away.

How many are left?

___ take away ___ is ___ .

There are 5 .

3 bounce away.

How many are left?

___ take away ___ is ___ .

There are 6 .

2 bounce away.

How many are left?

___ take away ___ is ___ .

There are 7 .

3 bounce away.

How many are left?

___ take away ___ is ___ .

There are 9 ⬤ .

2 ⬤ bounce away.

How many are left?

___ take away ___ is ___ .

There are 10 ⬤ .

5 ⬤ bounce away.

How many are left?

___ take away ___ is ___ .

There are 11 ⬤ .

6 ⬤ bounce away.

How many are left?

___ take away ___ is ___ .

There are 12 ⬤ .

7 ⬤ bounce away.

How many are left?

___ take away ___ is ___ .

Write your own maths story.

There are ☐ balls.

☐ balls bounce away.

How many are left?

☐ take away ☐ is ☐ .

Let's Count Back to Subtract

Use the number line.
Count back to subtract.
Write the difference.
The first one is done for you.

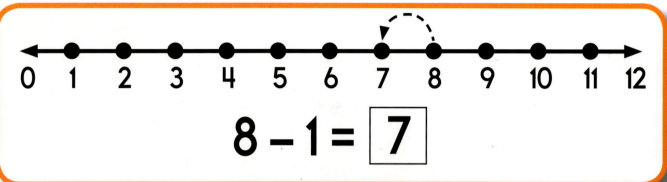

$$8 - 1 = \boxed{7}$$

$$9 - 1 = \square$$

$$8 - 2 = \square$$

$$\begin{array}{r} 12 \\ -1 \\ \hline \square \end{array}$$

$$\begin{array}{r} 3 \\ -1 \\ \hline \square \end{array}$$

$$\begin{array}{r} 5 \\ -1 \\ \hline \square \end{array}$$

$$\begin{array}{r} 7 \\ -2 \\ \hline \square \end{array}$$

$$\begin{array}{r} 6 \\ -2 \\ \hline \square \end{array}$$

$$\begin{array}{r} 4 \\ -2 \\ \hline \square \end{array}$$

$$\begin{array}{r} 11 \\ -2 \\ \hline \square \end{array}$$

Use the number line.
Count back to subtract.
Write the difference.

0 1 2 3 4 5 6 7 8 9 10 11 12

$$3 - 2 = \boxed{}$$

$$4 - 1 = \boxed{}$$

$$10 - 2 = \boxed{}$$

$$5 - 2 = \boxed{}$$

$$10 - 1 = \boxed{}$$

$$7 - 1 = \boxed{}$$

$$9 - 2 = \boxed{}$$

$$10 - 2 = \boxed{}$$

$$12 - 2 = \boxed{}$$

$$6 - 1 = \boxed{}$$

Let's Count Back to Subtract

Use the number line.
Count back to subtract.
Write the difference.

$$0 \quad 1 \quad 2 \quad 3 \quad 4 \quad 5 \quad 6 \quad 7 \quad 8 \quad 9 \quad 10 \quad 11 \quad 12$$

$9 - 3 = \boxed{}$

$11 - 1 = \boxed{}$

$12 - 2 = \boxed{}$

$8 - 3 = \boxed{}$

$10 - 3 = \boxed{}$

$11 - 2 = \boxed{}$

$$\begin{array}{r} 12 \\ -\ 3 \\ \hline \boxed{} \end{array}$$

$$\begin{array}{r} 8 \\ -\ 2 \\ \hline \boxed{} \end{array}$$

$$\begin{array}{r} 11 \\ -\ 3 \\ \hline \boxed{} \end{array}$$

$$\begin{array}{r} 10 \\ -\ 2 \\ \hline \boxed{} \end{array}$$

Let's Subtract Doubles

Subtract.
Write the difference.

1 – 1 = ☐

6 – 6 = ☐

3 – 3 = ☐

5 – 5 = ☐

$$\begin{array}{r} 7 \\ -7 \\ \hline \end{array}$$ ☐

$$\begin{array}{r} 2 \\ -2 \\ \hline \end{array}$$ ☐

$$\begin{array}{r} 4 \\ -4 \\ \hline \end{array}$$ ☐

$$\begin{array}{r} 8 \\ -8 \\ \hline \end{array}$$ ☐

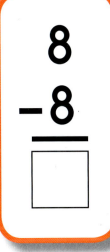

Let's Subtract 0

Subtract.
Write the difference.

$2 - 0 = \boxed{}$

$7 - 0 = \boxed{}$

$10 - 0 = \boxed{}$

$5 - 0 = \boxed{}$

$$\begin{array}{r} 4 \\ -\ 0 \\ \hline \boxed{} \end{array}$$

$$\begin{array}{r} 9 \\ -\ 0 \\ \hline \boxed{} \end{array}$$

$$\begin{array}{r} 11 \\ -\ 0 \\ \hline \boxed{} \end{array}$$

$$\begin{array}{r} 6 \\ -\ 0 \\ \hline \boxed{} \end{array}$$

Subtracting 0 does not change the number!

Let's Race

Solve the problems.
Record your time and the
number of correct answers.
On your mark, get set, go!

4 − 1	6 − 1	5 − 5	3 − 2	5 − 2
6 − 4	4 − 3	8 − 2	7 − 3	4 − 2
5 − 4	4 − 4	9 − 1	7 − 2	6 − 3
5 − 1	7 − 4	2 − 2	8 − 1	7 − 0
2 − 1	3 − 3	3 − 0		

Time to Complete: _____

Total Answers: _____

Total Correct: _____

Let's Learn Fact Families

Complete each fact family. The first one is done for you.

8 + 4 = 12   12 − 8 = 4

4 + 8 = 12   12 − 4 = 8

9 + 3 = ___   12 − ___ = 3

___ + 9 = 12   ___ − 3 = 9

7 + 4 = ___   11 − ___ = 4

___ + 7 = 11   ___ − 4 = 7

___ + 5 = ___   ___ − ___ = 5

___ + 7 = 12   ___ − ___ = 7

___ + ___ = ___   ___ − ___ = ___

___ + ___ = ___   ___ − ___ = ___

Let's Add and Subtract

Add or subtract.
Write the answers.
The first ones are done for you.

+2

add 2

IN	OUT
4	6
2	
8	
5	

take away 1

−1

IN	OUT
6	5
3	
9	
11	

Let's Race

Solve the problems.
Record your time and the
number of correct answers.
On your mark, get set, go!

7 + 2	8 − 5	6 − 5	9 + 2	9 + 0
6 − 4	2 + 8	10 − 3	3 + 3	7 − 1
10 − 10	4 + 5	5 + 4	9 − 9	5 + 6
8 + 4	5 − 3	3 + 6	8 − 0	9 − 7
4 − 2	2 + 2	8 − 8		

Time to Complete: _____

Total Answers: _____

Total Correct: _____

Solve the problems.
Record your time and the
number of correct answers.
On your mark, get set, go!

6 + 3	12 − 4	10 − 9	8 + 3	3 + 8
12 − 5	6 + 6	11 − 6	7 + 4	8 − 1
11 − 11	4 + 0	5 + 3	9 − 2	5 + 5
8 + 1	12 − 3	3 + 7	8 − 7	11 − 4
10 − 6	10 − 2	11 − 7		

Time to Complete: _____

Total Answers: _____

Total Correct: _____

Let's Count to Add and Subtract

1	2	3	4	5
6	7	8	9	10
11	12	13	14	15
16	17	18	19	20
21	22	23	24	25
26	27	28	29	30
31	32	33	34	35
36	37	38	39	40
41	42	43	44	45
46	47	48	49	50

Start at 5. Count up 3. Write the number.   _____

Start at 15. Count up 5. Write the number.   _____

Start at 25. Count back 2. Write the number.   _____

Start at 30. Count back 4. Write the number.   _____

Let's Count by 2s

Count by 2s.
Find the number stickers to fill in the missing numbers.

 2, 4, ⬜, 8, ⬜

 12, ⬜, 16, 18, ⬜

 ⬜, 24, ⬜, 28, ⬜

 32, ⬜, 36, ⬜, ⬜

 ⬜, 44, ⬜, 48, ⬜

Let's Count by 5s

Count by 5s.
Find the number stickers to fill in the missing numbers.

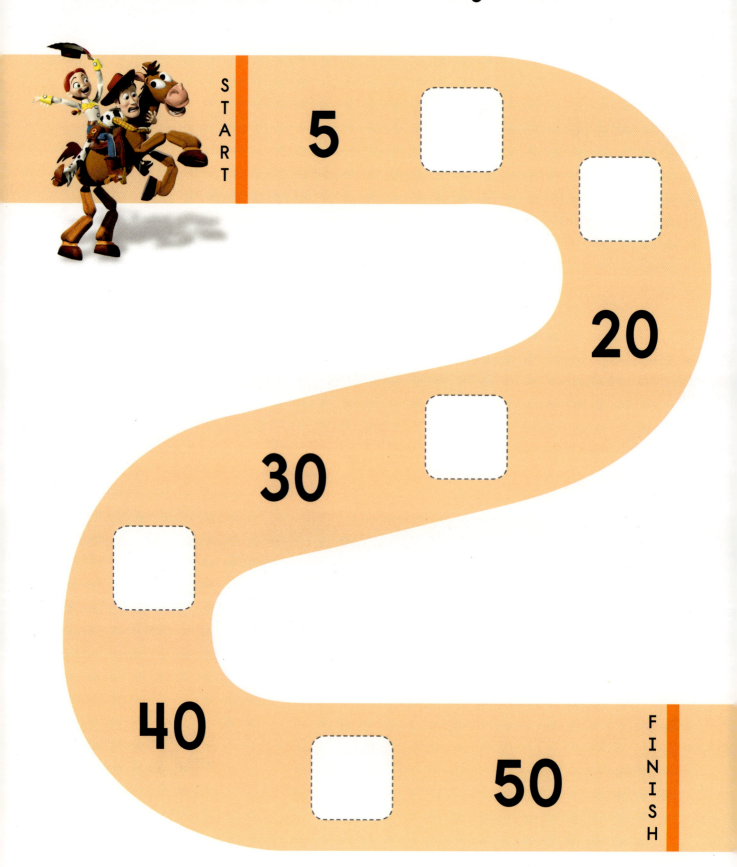

START

5

20

30

40

50

FINISH

Let's Count by 10s

Count by 10s.
Find the number stickers to fill in the missing numbers.

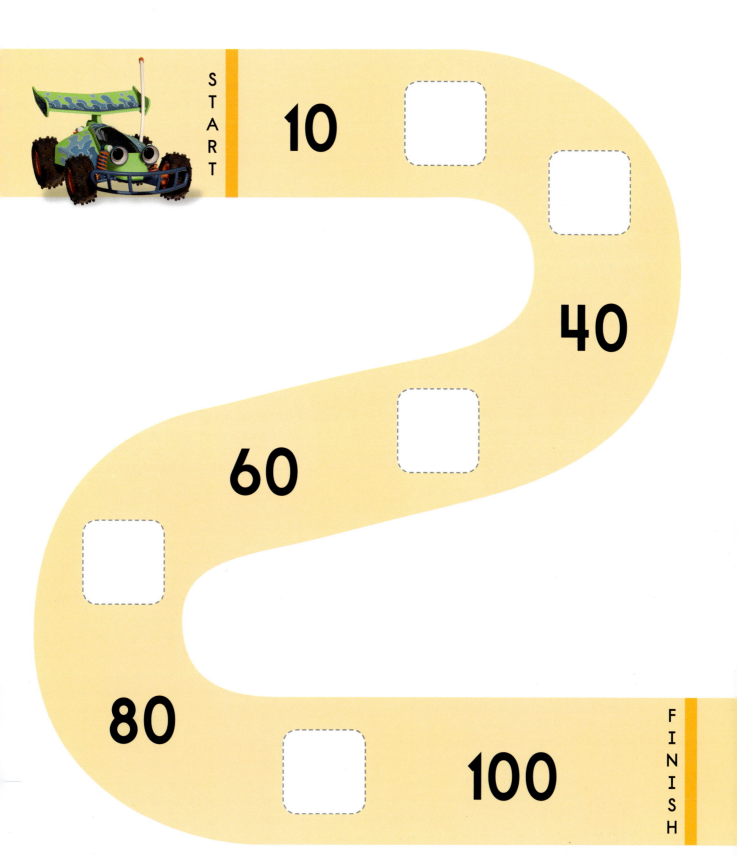

START

10

40

60

80

100

FINISH

Let's Count by 2s, 5s and 10s

1	2	3	4	5
6	7	8	9	10
11	12	13	14	15
16	17	18	19	20
21	22	23	24	25
26	27	28	29	30
31	32	33	34	35
36	37	38	39	40
41	42	43	44	45
46	47	48	49	50

Start at 2. Count by 2s to 10.
Write the numbers.

2 , ____ , ____ , ____ , ____

Start at 5. Count by 5s to 25.
Write the numbers.

5 , ____ , ____ , ____ , ____

Start at 10. Count by 10s to 50.
Write the numbers.

10 , ____ , ____ , ____ , ____

Let's Add Doubles

Add the doubles. Write the sum.

2 + 2 = ☐

4 + 4 = ☐

5 + 5 = ☐

3 + 3 = ☐

$$\begin{array}{r} 8 \\ +\,8 \\ \hline \square \end{array}$$

$$\begin{array}{r} 10 \\ +10 \\ \hline \square \end{array}$$

$$\begin{array}{r} 9 \\ +9 \\ \hline \square \end{array}$$

$$\begin{array}{r} 7 \\ +7 \\ \hline \square \end{array}$$

Try this:

8 + 8 = ☐   80 + 80 = ☐

Let's Add
Doubles Plus One

Add.
Use the doubles to help find the sum.

7 + 7 = ☐
7 + 8 = ☐

5 + 5 = ☐
5 + 6 = ☐

6 + 6 = ☐
6 + 7 = ☐

8 + 8 = ☐
8 + 9 = ☐

4
+5
☐

2
+3
☐

7
+6
☐

9
+8
☐

Let's Make 10

Add the checkers. Write the missing numbers.
The first one is done for you.

$8 + 3 = \underline{11}$

$10 + \underline{1} = \underline{11}$

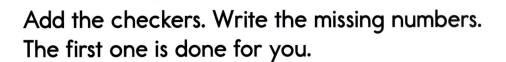

$9 + 4 = \underline{}$

$10 + \underline{} = \underline{}$

$8 + 4 = \underline{}$

$10 + \underline{} = \underline{}$

$6 + 7 = \underline{}$

$10 + \underline{} = \underline{}$

$7 + 7 = \underline{}$

$10 + \underline{} = \underline{}$

Let's Race

Solve the problems.
Record your time and the
number of correct answers.
On your mark, get set, go!

7 + 7	8 + 9	5 + 6	6 + 9	8 + 8
3 + 4	8 + 4	11 + 4	6 + 8	9 + 4
7 + 6	3 + 3	8 + 7	11 + 3	10 + 6
12 + 5	4 + 4	9 + 7	7 + 8	6 + 6
5 + 5	9 + 6	10 + 4		Time to Complete: _____ Total Answers: _____ Total Correct: _____

Solve the problems.
Record your time and the
number of correct answers.
On your mark, get set, go!

15 + 0	10 + 7	13 + 2	11 + 7	13 + 1
6 + 7	12 + 2	11 + 5	12 + 3	9 + 9
14 + 0	10 + 8	3 + 9	11 + 6	9 + 5
13 + 4	14 + 4	12 + 4	10 + 5	15 + 3
13 + 3	15 + 2	16 + 1		

Time to Complete: _____

Total Answers: _____

Total Correct: _____

Let's Use Doubles to Subtract

Subtract.
Write the difference.

14 – 7 = ▢

16 – 8 = ▢

18 – 9 = ▢

12 – 6 = ▢

$$\begin{array}{r} 6 \\ -3 \\ \hline \square \end{array}$$

$$\begin{array}{r} 2 \\ -1 \\ \hline \square \end{array}$$

$$\begin{array}{r} 10 \\ -5 \\ \hline \square \end{array}$$

$$\begin{array}{r} 8 \\ -4 \\ \hline \square \end{array}$$

Subtract.
Write the difference.

11 – 5 = ☐

13 – 8 = ☐

12 – 12 = ☐

16 – 7 = ☐

```
  14
-  5
-----
  ☐
```

```
  15
-  3
-----
  ☐
```

```
  17
-  6
-----
  ☐
```

```
  18
-  9
-----
  ☐
```

Let's Relate Addition and Subtraction Facts

Subtract.
Write the addition fact that helps.
The first one is done for you.

$$16 - 7 = \boxed{9}$$

$$7 + \boxed{9} = 16$$

$$18 - 9 = \boxed{}$$

$$9 + \boxed{} = 18$$

$$12 - 5 = \boxed{}$$

$$5 + \boxed{} = 12$$

$$17 - 9 = \boxed{}$$

$$9 + \boxed{} = 17$$

$$15 - 7 = \boxed{}$$

$$7 + \boxed{} = 15$$

Read the problem.
Write the number sentence.
The first one is done for you.

Woody scores 8 points.
Buzz scores 4 more.
How many points in all?

$$\underline{8} + \underline{4} = \underline{12}$$

Woody has 10 balloons.
7 balloons fly away.
How many are left?

$$\underline{} - \underline{} = \underline{}$$

Woody runs 12 laps.
Buzz runs 6 more.
How many laps in all?

$$\underline{} + \underline{} = \underline{}$$

Woody has 13 tickets.
He loses 7 tickets.
How many are left?

$$\underline{} - \underline{} = \underline{}$$

Buzz has 14 power bars.
He eats 6 power bars.
How many are left?

$$\underline{} - \underline{} = \underline{}$$

Answer Keys

Let's Show Different Ways to Make 7, 8, 9, 10, 11, 12

Answers will vary.
Possibilities include:

7	4 and 3	6 and 1
	5 and 2	7 and 0
8	4 and 4	7 and 1
	5 and 3	8 and 0
	6 and 2	
9	5 and 4	8 and 1
	6 and 3	9 and 0
	7 and 2	

Answers will vary.
Possibilities include:

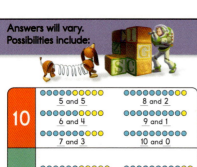

10	5 and 5	8 and 2
	6 and 4	9 and 1
	7 and 3	10 and 0
11	6 and 5	9 and 2
	7 and 4	10 and 1
	8 and 3	11 and 0
12	6 and 6	10 and 2
	7 and 5	11 and 1
	8 and 4	12 and 0
	9 and 3	

Let's Add

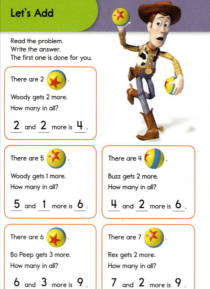

Read the problem.
Write the answer.
The first one is done for you.

There are 2 ⭐.
Woody gets 2 more.
How many in all?

2 and 2 more is 4.

There are 5 ⭐.
Woody gets 1 more.
How many in all?

5 and 1 more is 6.

There are 4 🏐.
Buzz gets 2 more.
How many in all?

4 and 2 more is 6.

There are 6 ⭐.
Bo Peep gets 3 more.
How many in all?

6 and 3 more is 9.

There are 7 ⭐.
Rex gets 2 more.
How many in all?

7 and 2 more is 9.

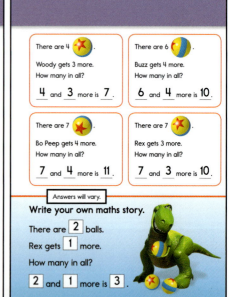

There are 4 ⭐.
Woody gets 3 more.
How many in all?

4 and 3 more is 7.

There are 6 🏐.
Buzz gets 4 more.
How many in all?

6 and 4 more is 10.

There are 7 🏐.
Bo Peep gets 4 more.
How many in all?

7 and 4 more is 11.

There are 7 🏐.
Rex gets 3 more.
How many in all?

7 and 3 more is 10.

Answers will vary.

Write your own maths story.

There are 2 balls.
Rex gets 1 more.
How many in all?

2 and 1 more is 3.

Let's Count On to Add

4 plus 3.
Start at 4.
Count on 3:
4 . . . 5, 6, 7

Count on to add.
Write the sum.
The first one is done for you.

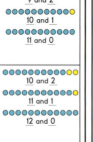

4 + 3 = 7

6 + 2 = 8   3 + 2 = 5

$$\begin{array}{r}4\\+2\\\hline 6\end{array}$$ $$\begin{array}{r}5\\+1\\\hline 6\end{array}$$ $$\begin{array}{r}3\\+3\\\hline 6\end{array}$$

(Use the number line)

Use the number line.
Count on to add.
Write the sum.

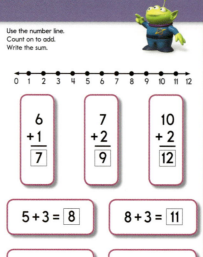

$$\begin{array}{r}6\\+1\\\hline 7\end{array}$$ $$\begin{array}{r}7\\+2\\\hline 9\end{array}$$ $$\begin{array}{r}10\\+2\\\hline 12\end{array}$$

5 + 3 = 8   8 + 3 = 11

9 + 3 = 12   11 + 1 = 12

Let's Add 0

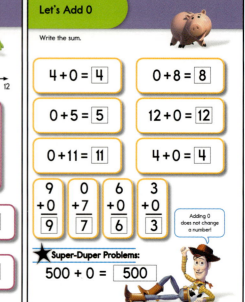

Write the sum.

4 + 0 = 4   0 + 8 = 8

0 + 5 = 5   12 + 0 = 12

0 + 11 = 11   4 + 0 = 4

$$\begin{array}{r}9\\+0\\\hline 9\end{array}$$ $$\begin{array}{r}0\\+7\\\hline 7\end{array}$$ $$\begin{array}{r}6\\+0\\\hline 6\end{array}$$ $$\begin{array}{r}3\\+0\\\hline 3\end{array}$$

Adding 0 does not change a number!

★ **Super-Duper Problems:**

500 + 0 = 500

Let's Add Doubles

Write the sum.

0 + 0 = [0]	2 + 2 = [4]
3 + 3 = [6]	4 + 4 = [8]
6 + 6 = [12]	8 + 8 = [16]

5 +5 10	7 +7 14	9 +9 18	10 +10 20

⭐ **Super-Duper Problems:**

100 + 100 = [200]

1000 + 1000 = [2000]

Let's Add with 5

Add the checkers.
Write the sum.
The first one is done for you.

5 + 3 = 8

5 + 1 = 6   5 + 2 = 7

5 + 4 = 9   5 + 0 = 5

Let's Add

Color the checkers.
Write the sum.
The first one is done for you.

6 + 2 = 8

7 + 1 = 8   6 + 3 = 9

8 + 1 = 9   7 + 2 = 9

Let's Race

Solve the problems.
Record your time and the number of correct answers.
On your mark, get set, go!

6 + 4 10	7 + 3 10	5 + 6 11	2 + 9 11	4 + 2 6
3 + 3 6	8 + 4 12	3 + 6 9	6 + 3 9	0 + 8 8
9 + 3 12	6 + 6 12	8 + 3 11	2 + 3 5	7 + 2 9
1 + 3 4	6 + 0 6	3 + 4 7	3 + 2 5	1 + 7 8
6 + 2 8	4 + 5 9	10 + 2 12	Time to Complete: ____ Total Answers: ____ Total Correct: ____

Solve the problems.
Record your time and the number of correct answers.
On your mark, get set, go!

4 + 1 5	7 + 5 12	0 + 2 2	2 + 4 6	3 + 0 3
4 + 7 11	2 + 7 9	1 + 6 7	4 + 3 7	8 + 1 9
1 + 1 2	8 + 2 10	5 + 3 8	7 + 4 11	2 + 2 4
5 + 5 10	1 + 2 3	5 + 7 12	4 + 6 10	0 + 7 7
10 + 1 11	5 + 1 6	4 + 4 8	Time to Complete: ____ Total Answers: ____ Total Correct: ____

Let's Subtract

Read the problem.
Write the difference.
The first one is done for you.

There are 3 ⭐.
2 ⭐ bounce away.
How many are left?
3 take away 2 is 1.

There are 4 ⭐.
2 ⭐ bounce away.
How many are left?
4 take away 2 is 2.

There are 5 🏐.
3 🏐 bounce away.
How many are left?
5 take away 3 is 2.

There are 6 ⭐.
2 ⭐ bounce away.
How many are left?
6 take away 2 is 4.

There are 7 ⭐.
3 ⭐ bounce away.
How many are left?
7 take away 3 is 4.

There are 9 ⭐.
2 ⭐ bounce away.
How many are left?
9 take away 2 is 7.

There are 10 🏐.
5 🏐 bounce away.
How many are left?
10 take away 5 is 5.

There are 11 🏐.
6 🏐 bounce away.
How many are left?
11 take away 6 is 5.

There are 12 ⭐.
7 ⭐ bounce away.
How many are left?
12 take away 7 is 5.

Answers will vary.

Write your own maths story.

There are [5] balls.
[2] balls bounce away.
How many are left?
[5] take away [2] is [3].

Let's Count Back to Subtract

Use the number line.
Count back to subtract.
Write the difference.
The first one is done for you.

0 1 2 3 4 5 6 7 8 9 10 11 12
8 – 1 = [7]

9 – 1 = [8]	12 – 1 [11]	3 – 1 [2]
8 – 2 = [6]		

5 – 1 [4]	7 – 2 [5]	6 – 2 [4]	4 – 2 [2]	11 – 2 [9]

Use the number line.
Count back to subtract.
Write the difference.

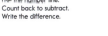
0 1 2 3 4 5 6 7 8 9 10 11 12

3 – 2 [1]	4 – 1 [3]	10 – 2 [8]	5 – 2 [3]

10 – 1 = [9]	7 – 1 = [6]
9 – 2 = [7]	10 – 2 = [8]
12 – 2 = [10]	6 – 1 = [5]

Let's Count Back to Subtract

Use the number line.
Count back to subtract.
Write the difference.

0 1 2 3 4 5 6 7 8 9 10 11 12

9 − 3 = 6	11 − 1 = 10
12 − 2 = 10	8 − 3 = 5
10 − 3 = 7	11 − 2 = 9

| 12 −3 = 9 | 8 −2 = 6 | 11 −3 = 8 | 10 −2 = 8 |

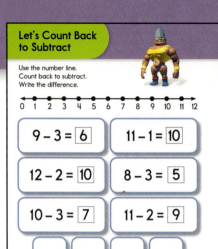

Let's Subtract Doubles

Subtract.
Write the difference.

| 1 − 1 = 0 | 6 − 6 = 0 |
| 3 − 3 = 0 | 5 − 5 = 0 |

| 7 −7 = 0 | 2 −2 = 0 | 4 −4 = 0 | 8 −8 = 0 |

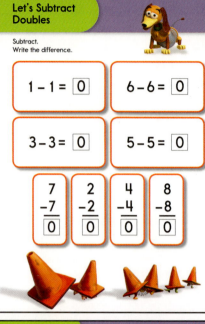

Let's Subtract 0

Subtract.
Write the difference.

| 2 − 0 = 2 | 7 − 0 = 7 |
| 10 − 0 = 10 | 5 − 0 = 5 |

| 4 −0 = 4 | 9 −0 = 9 | 11 −0 = 11 | 6 −0 = 6 |

Subtracting 0 does not change the number!

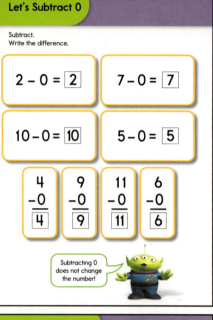

Let's Race

Solve the problems.
Record your time and the number of correct answers.
On your mark, get set, go!

4 −1 = 3	6 −1 = 5	5 −5 = 0	3 −2 = 1	5 −2 = 3
6 −4 = 2	4 −3 = 1	8 −2 = 6	7 −3 = 4	4 −2 = 2
5 −4 = 1	4 −4 = 0	9 −1 = 8	7 −2 = 5	6 −3 = 3
5 −1 = 4	7 −4 = 3	2 −2 = 0	8 −1 = 7	7 −0 = 7
2 −1 = 1	3 −3 = 0	3 −0 = 3		

Time to Complete: _____
Total Answers: _____
Total Correct: _____

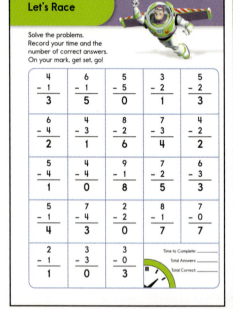

Let's Learn Fact Families

Complete each fact family.
The first one is done for you.

| 8 + 4 = 12 | 12 − 8 = 4 |
| 4 + 8 = 12 | 12 − 4 = 8 |

| 9 + 3 = 12 | 12 − 9 = 3 |
| 3 + 9 = 12 | 12 − 3 = 9 |

| 7 + 4 = 11 | 11 − 7 = 4 |
| 4 + 7 = 11 | 11 − 4 = 7 |

| 7 + 5 = 12 | 12 − 7 = 5 |
| 5 + 7 = 12 | 12 − 5 = 7 |

| 9 + 5 = 14 | 14 − 5 = 9 |
| 5 + 9 = 14 | 14 − 9 = 5 |

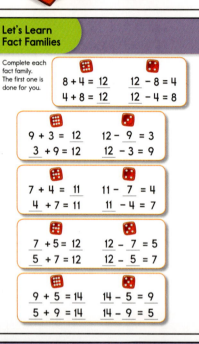

Let's Add and Subtract

Add or subtract.
Write the answers.
The first ones are done for you.

add 2

+2

IN	OUT
4	6
2	4
8	10
5	7

take away 1

−1

IN	OUT
6	5
3	2
9	8
11	10

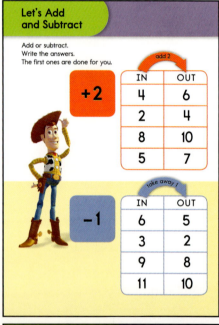

Let's Race

Solve the problems.
Record your time and the number of correct answers.
On your mark, get set, go!

7 +2 = 9	8 −5 = 3	6 −5 = 1	9 +2 = 11	9 +0 = 9
6 −4 = 2	2 +8 = 10	10 −3 = 7	3 +3 = 6	7 −1 = 6
10 −10 = 0	4 +5 = 9	5 +4 = 9	9 −9 = 0	5 +6 = 11
8 +4 = 12	5 −3 = 2	3 +6 = 9	8 −0 = 8	9 −7 = 2
4 −2 = 2	2 +2 = 4	8 −8 = 0		

Time to Complete: _____
Total Answers: _____
Total Correct: _____

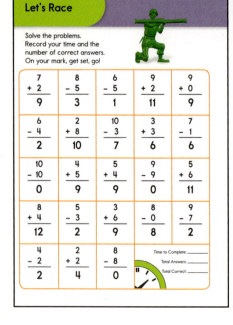

Let's Race

Solve the problems.
Record your time and the number of correct answers.
On your mark, get set, go!

6 +3 = 9	12 −4 = 8	10 −9 = 1	8 +3 = 11	3 +8 = 11
12 −5 = 7	6 +6 = 12	11 −6 = 5	7 +4 = 11	8 −1 = 7
11 −11 = 0	4 +0 = 4	5 +3 = 8	9 −2 = 7	5 +5 = 10
8 +1 = 9	12 −3 = 9	3 +7 = 10	8 −7 = 1	11 −4 = 7
10 −6 = 4	10 −2 = 8	11 −7 = 4		

Time to Complete: _____
Total Answers: _____
Total Correct: _____

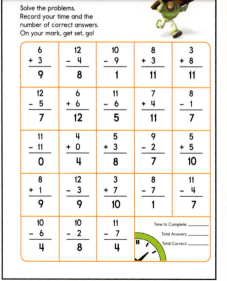

Let's Count to Add and Subtract

1	2	3	4	5
6	7	8	9	10
11	12	13	14	15
16	17	18	19	20
21	22	23	24	25
26	27	28	29	30
31	32	33	34	35
36	37	38	39	40
41	42	43	44	45
46	47	48	49	50

Start at 5. Count up 3. Write the number. __8__

Start at 15. Count up 5. Write the number. __20__

Start at 25. Count back 2. Write the number. __23__

Start at 30. Count back 4. Write the number. __26__

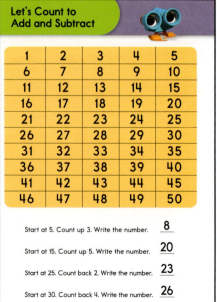

Let's Count by 2s

Count by 2s.
Find the number stickers to fill in the missing numbers.

2, 4, 6, 8, 10

12, 14, 16, 18, 20

22, 24, 26, 28, 30

32, 34, 36, 38, 40

42, 44, 46, 48, 50

Let's Count by 10s

Count by 10s.
Find the number stickers to fill in the missing numbers.

START 10 20 30 40 50 60 70 80 90 100 FINISH

Let's Count by 5s

Count by 5s.
Find the number stickers to fill in the missing numbers.

START 5 10 15 20 25 30 35 40 45 50 FINISH

Let's Count by 2s, 5s and 10s

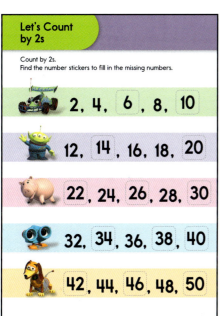

1	2	3	4	5
6	7	8	9	10
11	12	13	14	15
16	17	18	19	20
21	22	23	24	25
26	27	28	29	30
31	32	33	34	35
36	37	38	39	40
41	42	43	44	45
46	47	48	49	50

Start at 2. Count by 2s to 10.
Write the numbers.   2 4 6 8 10

Start at 5. Count by 5s to 25.
Write the numbers.   5 10 15 20 25

Start at 10. Count by 10s to 50.
Write the numbers.   10 20 30 40 50

Let's Add Doubles

Add the doubles. Write the sum.

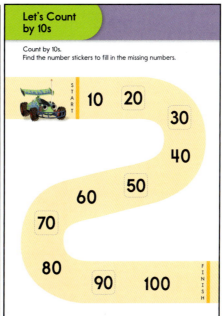

2 + 2 = 4

4 + 4 = 8

5 + 5 = 10

3 + 3 = 6

8
+8
16

10
+10
20

9
+9
18

7
+7
14

Try this:

8 + 8 = 16   80 + 80 = 160

Let's Add Doubles Plus One

Add.
Use the doubles to help find the sum.

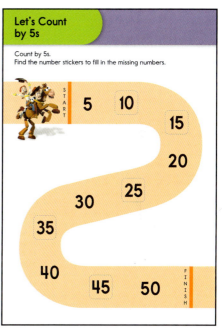

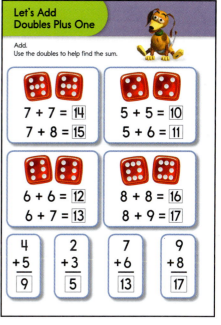

7 + 7 = 14
7 + 8 = 15

5 + 5 = 10
5 + 6 = 11

6 + 6 = 12
6 + 7 = 13

8 + 8 = 16
8 + 9 = 17

4
+5
9

2
+3
5

7
+6
13

9
+8
17

Let's Make 10

Add the checkers. Write the missing numbers. The first one is done for you.

$8 + 3 = 11$
$10 + 1 = 11$

$9 + 4 = 13$
$10 + 3 = 13$

$8 + 4 = 12$
$10 + 2 = 12$

$6 + 7 = 13$
$10 + 3 = 13$

$7 + 7 = 14$
$10 + 4 = 14$

Let's Race

Solve the problems. Record your time and the number of correct answers. On your mark, get set, go!

7 + 7 14	8 + 9 17	5 + 6 11	6 + 9 15	8 + 8 16
3 + 4 7	8 + 4 12	11 + 4 15	6 + 8 14	9 + 4 13
7 + 6 13	3 + 3 6	8 + 7 15	11 + 3 14	10 + 6 16
12 + 5 17	4 + 4 8	9 + 7 16	7 + 8 15	6 + 6 12
5 + 5 10	9 + 6 15	10 + 4 14	Time to Complete: _____ Total Answers: _____ Total Correct: _____	

Let's Race

Solve the problems. Record your time and the number of correct answers. On your mark, get set, go!

15 + 0 15	10 + 7 17	13 + 2 15	11 + 7 18	13 + 1 14
6 + 7 13	12 + 2 14	11 + 5 16	12 + 3 15	9 + 9 18
14 + 0 14	10 + 8 18	3 + 9 12	11 + 6 17	9 + 5 14
13 + 4 17	14 + 4 18	12 + 4 16	10 + 5 15	15 + 3 18
13 + 3 16	15 + 2 17	16 + 1 17	Time to Complete: _____ Total Answers: _____ Total Correct: _____	

Let's Use Doubles to Subtract

Subtract. Write the difference.

 $14 - 7 = 7$

$16 - 8 = 8$

 $18 - 9 = 9$

$12 - 6 = 6$

6 − 3 3	2 − 1 1
10 − 5 5	8 − 4 4

Let's Learn Subtraction Facts

Subtract. Write the difference.

$11 - 5 = 6$ $13 - 8 = 5$

$12 - 12 = 0$ $16 - 7 = 9$

14 − 5 9	15 − 3 12
17 − 6 11	18 − 9 9

Let's Relate Addition and Subtraction Facts

Subtract. Write the addition fact that helps. The first one is done for you.

16 − 7 9	7 + 9 16

18 − 9 9	9 + 9 18	12 − 5 7	5 + 7 12

17 − 9 8	9 + 8 17	15 − 7 8	7 + 8 15

Let's Solve Word Problems

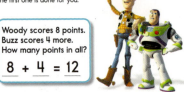

Read the problem. Write the number sentence. The first one is done for you.

Woody scores 8 points. Buzz scores 4 more. How many points in all?
$8 + 4 = 12$

Woody has 10 balloons. 7 balloons fly away. How many are left?
$10 - 7 = 3$

Woody runs 12 laps. Buzz runs 6 more. How many laps in all?
$12 + 6 = 18$

Woody has 13 tickets. He loses 7 tickets. How many are left?
$13 - 7 = 6$

Buzz has 14 power bars. He eats 6 power bars. How many are left?
$14 - 6 = 8$